The start of Love

LOIS WYSE

American Greetings Corporation
Cleveland, Ohio 44144

Published by American Greetings, American Road, Cleveland, Ohio 4414◦
First printing, June, 1971. Copyright, 1971, by Lois Wyse.
Library of Congress Catalogue Card Number: 78-157564
Printed in the United States of America
An American Greetings Book

From a <u>slow</u> <u>starter.</u>

Feb 14, 1974

The Start of Love

To pass the point of bitterness
Is to reach the start of love.

On Meeting a New Man

It is one thing to know you could love him,
Another to know if you should.

Should you?

Vocabulary of Love

In one look can be
The whole vocabulary
Of love.

So think well
Before you look at me.

That's the look of "oneness"

Directional

Love is not where we started.
Love is where we are going.

Who is to judge good or bad?

Hey, Look at Me

Looking at you
Does not make me
Know you better.

Even so,
I like
Looking at you.

me too!

Encore! Encore!

Some days should be held over
By popular demand.

Every one of our moments together!

New Love

New love is like typing
On white paper.
Who will strike
The ~~fone~~ first key,
The ~~rice and~~ right key?

Trial and error.
That is love.

I'm frightened of that.

Color Blind

The presence of you
Has colored my life
Not in
Reds and yellows
That I understand
But in taupes and mauves
And orange gold sunsets
That defy interpretation.

Local Casanova

They say he's marvelous with women.
But how do you think he is with a woman?

Depends ? ? ?

Tough Fight

The things
I do not like in you
Are the things
I fight in me.
But when I battle them
In you,
It is easier to win.

The Shape of Love to Come

I want us to be
What our love makes us.
Forget the goals and plans.
Let us be shaped
By the love we shape.

A Prayer for Us

Instead of anger
Let me feel
Compassion.

Instead of rage
Let me show
Concern.

Instead of hate
Let me seek
Change.

> For, if
> To a warring, wondering world
> Each of us will bring

Compassion
Concern
Change

> Then perhaps there will be

Love.

AMEN!

The Author

Lois Wyse is the author of best-selling books of
love poetry, including "Love Poems For The Very Married",
"Are You Sure You Love Me?", and "I Love You Better Now",
as well as the popular non-fiction book, "Mrs. Success".
Her articles and poems appear regularly in numerous
magazines in the United States and abroad.

Lois Wyse, her husband Marc, and their two children,
Katherine and Robert, live in Shaker Heights, Ohio.